101 FACTS

ABOUT

Taylor Swift

Quizzes, Quotes, Journals and More!

Intro to
Taylor Swift

Taylor Swift is a global icon whose name has become synonymous with modern pop music. Born on December 13, 1989, in Reading, Pennsylvania, Swift's journey to stardom began at a young age. Growing up on a Christmas tree farm, she developed a passion for music and began performing in local talent shows and events.

At the age of 14, Swift convinced her family to relocate to Nashville, Tennessee, the epicenter of country music, to pursue her dreams of becoming a singer-songwriter. Despite facing initial rejections from record labels, her determination and talent caught the attention of Scott Borchetta, founder of Big Machine Records, who signed her to the label.

In 2006, Swift released her self-titled debut album, which catapulted her into the spotlight with hits like "Tim McGraw" and "Teardrops on My Guitar." Since then, she has become one of the best-selling music artists of all time, known for her honest and relatable songwriting, captivating performances, and ability to constantly reinvent herself.

From country sweetheart to pop sensation, Swift has seamlessly transitioned between genres, earning critical acclaim and numerous awards along the way, including 11 Grammy Awards. Beyond her musical achievements, she is also recognized for her philanthropy, activism, and influence on pop culture.

With her unmistakable talent, unwavering authenticity, and unparalleled success, Taylor Swift continues to inspire and captivate audiences worldwide, solidifying her legacy as one of the most influential artists of her generation.

Cats, Coffee, and Cardigans: A Day in the Life of Taylor Swift

1. Paws and Purrs: A Glimpse into Taylor's Feline Family

Taylor Swift's world is often accompanied by the playful pitter-patter of paws and the soft purring of her two adorable Scottish Fold cats, Olivia Benson and Meredith Grey. Named after characters from popular TV shows, these furry companions have become staples in Taylor's life, providing her with endless love and companionship. Whether it's snuggling up on the couch while Taylor strums her guitar or making cameo appearances in her Instagram posts, Olivia and Meredith are more than just pets—they're cherished members of the Swift family.

2. Brewing Creativity: Taylor's Love Affair with Coffee

As the sun rises over Nashville, Taylor Swift's day begins with the comforting aroma of freshly brewed coffee. A self-proclaimed coffee enthusiast, Taylor takes her morning cup of joe seriously, often experimenting with different brewing methods and specialty blends. Whether she's sipping on a steaming latte while writing lyrics or grabbing a quick espresso before a recording session, coffee plays a vital role in fueling Taylor's creativity and sparking inspiration. With every sip, Taylor finds solace in the rich, complex flavors of her favorite brews, setting the stage for a day filled with music, magic, and endless possibilities.

3. Cozy Couture: Taylor's Signature Cardigan Collection

When it comes to fashion, Taylor Swift has mastered the art of effortless elegance, and her extensive collection of cozy cardigans is no exception. From chunky knits to lightweight cashmere, Taylor's wardrobe is brimming with an array of cardigan styles, each carefully curated to reflect her signature aesthetic. Whether she's running errands around town or attending star-studded events, Taylor effortlessly elevates her look with the addition of a classic cardigan, exuding timeless sophistication and undeniable charm. With their soft textures and versatile designs, Taylor's cardigans serve as the perfect complement to her laid-back yet polished sense of style, proving that comfort and fashion can coexist in perfect harmony.

4. Morning Melodies: Taylor's Wake-Up Playlist

As the first rays of sunlight filter through her window, Taylor Swift begins her day with the soothing sounds of her carefully curated wake-up playlist. Filled with an eclectic mix of tunes ranging from indie folk to pop anthems, Taylor's morning melodies set the tone for a day filled with creativity and inspiration. From uplifting ballads to soul-stirring ballads, each song on Taylor's playlist holds a special place in her heart, serving as a source of comfort and motivation as she embarks on another day in the spotlight. With every note and lyric, Taylor finds solace in the power of music, allowing it to guide her through the highs and lows of life with grace, resilience, and unwavering determination.

- Taylor Alison Swift was born on December 13, 1989, in Reading, Pennsylvania.

- She spent her early years on a Christmas tree farm in Pennsylvania before moving to Nashville, Tennessee, at the age of 14 to pursue a career in country music.

- Taylor Swift signed her first record deal with Big Machine Records when she was just 15 years old.

- Her self-titled debut album, "Taylor Swift," was released in 2006 and peaked at number five on the Billboard 200 chart.
- Swift is known for writing most of her own songs, drawing inspiration from her personal life experiences.

Easter Eggs and Hidden Gems: Decoding Taylor Swift's Music Videos

Taylor Swift's music videos are like a journey through a magical world full of surprises and hidden treasures! Just like exploring a mysterious cave in a video game, Taylor hides little secrets, called Easter eggs, in her videos that are super fun to discover.

In each of Taylor's music videos, she doesn't just tell a story with words and music, but also with pictures! As you watch, you might notice cool things happening in the background, special outfits Taylor wears, or even secret messages hidden in the scenes.

For example, let's take a look at Taylor's video for "Blank Space." At first glance, it might seem like Taylor is just having fun in a fancy mansion. But if you look closely, you'll notice that the mansion is filled with all kinds of interesting things. There are paintings and decorations that remind us of famous stories and artwork from history. It's like a magical mansion with secrets waiting to be discovered around every corner!

And in Taylor's video for "You Belong with Me," she plays two characters who are very different from each other. But if you pay close attention, you'll see how these characters are connected and learn important lessons about friendship and being true to yourself.

But what's even more exciting is how Taylor connects her videos together, like pieces of a puzzle! Sometimes, she'll leave a clue about her next song or album in one video that you won't notice until you watch the next one. It's like going on a big adventure with Taylor, and you never know what surprises you might find along the way!

So, the next time you watch a Taylor Swift music video, keep your eyes peeled for Easter eggs and hidden gems. You'll be amazed at all the secrets waiting to be discovered!

- Swift's album "Fearless" (2008) won the Grammy Award for Album of the Year, making her the youngest recipient of the award at the time.
- She is one of the best-selling music artists of all time, with numerous awards, including 11 Grammy Awards.
- Taylor Swift became the youngest artist to win the Country Music Association (CMA) Award for Entertainer of the Year in 2009.

Did You Know ?

- In 2014, she transitioned from country to pop music with her album "1989," which won Album of the Year at the Grammy Awards.

- Swift is also an accomplished actress, appearing in films such as "Valentine's Day" (2010) and "The Giver" (2014).

Letter to Taylor: Write a letter to
Taylor Swift expressing your
appreciation for her music and how
it has impacted your life. Share
personal stories or memories
related to her songs.

Date:

_____

_____

_____

_____

_____

_____

_____

_____

_____

_____

_____

_____

_____

_____

_____

_____

- She has a strong presence on social media, with millions of followers on platforms like Instagram, Twitter, and TikTok.
- Taylor Swift is known for her philanthropy, donating to various causes and charities, including disaster relief efforts and education programs.
- She has been an advocate for artists' rights and has spoken out against issues such as music streaming royalties.

- Swift has a close relationship with her fans, often interacting with them on social media and hosting secret listening sessions for new music.

- She has a collection of cats named after characters from TV shows and movies, including Olivia Benson and Meredith Grey.

PRODUCTION
SCENE | TAKE
DIRECTOR
CAMERA
DATE

1. What is the title of Taylor Swift's first single, released in 2006?
A) "Love Story"
B) "Tim McGraw"
 C) "You Belong with Me"
 D) "Shake It Off"

2. Which of the following albums by Taylor Swift won the Album of the Year award at the Grammy Awards?
A) "Red"
B) "Fearless"
C) "Speak Now"
D) "Lover"

3. Taylor Swift made her acting debut in which film?
A) "The Hunger Games"
B) "Pitch Perfect 2"
C) "The Giver"
D) "Valentine's Day"

- Taylor Swift is known for her signature red lipstick and vintage-inspired fashion sense.

- She has been involved in several high-profile romantic relationships, which often inspire her songwriting.

- Swift's song "Love Story" (2008) became one of her most successful singles and is considered one of the best-selling singles of all time.

- She has collaborated with artists from various genres, including Ed Sheeran, Kendrick Lamar, and Brendon Urie.

- Swift has received criticism and praise for her outspokenness on political and social issues, including civil rights and feminism.

"FEARLESS IS GETTING BACK UP AND FIGHTING FOR WHAT YOU WANT OVER AND OVER AGAIN... EVEN THOUGH EVERY TIME YOU'VE TRIED BEFORE, YOU'VE LOST."

- Taylor Swift

Did You Know ?

- Taylor Swift has a keen interest in literature and has referenced classic novels and poetry in her song lyrics.

- She has been honored with numerous awards for her songwriting abilities, including the Songwriter Icon Award from the National Music Publishers Association.

- She has performed at major events and venues worldwide, including the Super Bowl halftime show and Madison Square Garden.

- Swift's album "Red" (2012) featured collaborations with several renowned songwriters and producers, including Max Martin and Shellback.

- She has released multiple fragrance lines and has appeared in advertising campaigns for brands such as CoverGirl and Keds.

Inspired by Taylor: Taylor Swift inspires people with her music. Write about something you've done that you feel proud of, inspired by Taylor's messages of kindness and confidence.

Date:

_____

_____

_____

_____

_____

_____

_____

_____

_____

_____

_____

_____

_____

_____

_____

_____

1. Which of the following albums by Taylor Swift features the song "Love Story"?
A) "Speak Now"
B) "Fearless"
C) "1989"
D) "Red"

2. Taylor Swift won the Song of the Year Grammy Award for which of the following songs?
A) "Shake It Off"
B) "You Belong with Me"
C) "Mean"
D) "Blank Space"

3. Which of the following movies did Taylor Swift voice a character in?
A) "Frozen"
B) "Tangled"
C) "The Lorax"
D) "Moana"

Answers:
1. B) "Fearless"
2. C) "Mean"
3. C) "The Lorax"

- Taylor Swift's documentary film "Miss Americana" (2020) provided an intimate look at her life and career, addressing topics such as body image and fame.
- She has been recognized for her songwriting prowess by organizations such as the Nashville Songwriters Hall of Fame.
- Swift's album "Speak Now" (2010) was entirely self-written and showcased her storytelling abilities.

- Taylor Swift's song "Shake It Off" (2014) became an anthem for self-empowerment and resilience.
- She has won multiple American Music Awards, including Artist of the Decade in 2019.

"YOU CAN'T HAVE A BETTER TOMORROW IF YOU'RE STILL THINKING ABOUT YESTERDAY."

- Taylor Swift

Did You Know ?

- She has a loyal fanbase known as "Swifties," who are dedicated to supporting her music and career.
- Swift has headlined several world tours, including the "Speak Now World Tour" and the "Reputation Stadium Tour."
- She has been featured on the cover of numerous magazines, including Vogue, Rolling Stone, and Time.

Did You Know ?

- Taylor Swift's album "folklore" (2020) was released during the COVID-19 pandemic and received widespread critical acclaim.
- She has won multiple MTV Video Music Awards for her music videos, including "Bad Blood" and "You Need to Calm Down."

1. Which of the following Taylor Swift albums features the hit single "Shake It Off"?

A) "Red"

B) "Fearless"

C) "1989"

D) "Speak Now"

2. In which year did Taylor Swift release her album "Speak Now"?

A) 2008

B) 2010

C) 2012

D) 2014

3. Taylor Swift won her 3rd Album of the Year Grammy Award for which album?

A) "Red"

B) "Speak Now"

C) "Fearless"

D) "Folklore"

- Swift has been praised for her songwriting versatility, spanning genres such as country, pop, and indie folk.

- She is one of the best-selling digital music artists, with multiple singles certified multi-platinum.

- Taylor Swift's song "Blank Space" (2014) satirized media perceptions of her love life and received critical acclaim.

- She has collaborated with fashion designers and brands to create merchandise and clothing lines inspired by her music.
- Swift has been honored with the Grammy Award for Album of the Year three times, making her the first woman to achieve this feat.

"PEOPLE HAVEN'T ALWAYS BEEN THERE FOR ME, BUT MUSIC ALWAYS HAS."

- Taylor Swift

Did You Know ?

- She has used her platform to advocate for the rights of songwriters and musicians in the digital age.
- Taylor Swift's album "evermore" (2020) was released as a surprise companion to "folklore" and further explored themes of storytelling and imagination.
- She has performed at major music festivals, including Glastonbury and Coachella.

- Swift has won multiple Billboard Music Awards for her chart-topping albums and singles.
- She has a strong presence in the fashion industry and has been praised for her red carpet style.

WORD SEARCH

F	I	F	I	S	L	A	A	T	O	L	M	L	T
F	O	T	A	Y	L	O	R	A	E	E	I	H	G
H	E	N	C	H	A	N	T	E	D	R	D	M	E
R	N	H	I	R	A	T	I	U	G	O	N	N	E
R	R	A	T	A	A	S	A	O	Y	L	I	R	M
S	E	M	S	W	I	F	T	I	E	K	G	T	I
A	S	P	A	H	S	I	G	R	S	L	H	E	O
Y	E	E	U	A	V	Y	D	E	A	O	T	A	W
M	W	L	L	T	E	I	F	D	T	F	S	R	R
M	F	S	R	R	A	I	L	A	L	F	A	D	I
A	I	H	E	F	A	T	R	L	R	T	E	R	R
R	H	I	R	T	E	E	I	P	E	E	A	O	E
G	L	D	F	T	P	H	F	O	L	C	O	P	D
D	I	T	R	R	U	I	T	A	N	C	O	S	R

Reputation   Folklore   Nashville

Grammy Swiftie   Taylor   Enchanted

Midnights   Red Teardrops   Guitar   Fearless

Did You Know ?

- Taylor Swift's song "We Are Never Ever Getting Back Together" (2012) became her first number-one single on the Billboard Hot 100 chart.
- She has won the Brit Award for International Female Solo Artist multiple times.
- Swift has been involved in advocacy efforts to combat sexual assault and harassment in the music industry.

- She has released multiple concert films and documentaries, giving fans behind-the-scenes glimpses into her life as a musician.

- Taylor Swift's music has been praised for its relatability and emotional depth, resonating with listeners of all ages and backgrounds.

"HAPPINESS AND CONFIDENCE ARE THE PRETTIEST THINGS YOU CAN WEAR."

- Taylor Swift

- Taylor Swift has a strong presence on YouTube, with billions of views on her music videos and live performances.

- She has won numerous Country Music Association (CMA) Awards, including Song of the Year and Female Vocalist of the Year.

- Swift's album "Reputation" (2017) addressed themes of reputation, media scrutiny, and personal growth.

- She has been recognized by Forbes as one of the highest-paid celebrities multiple times.

- Taylor Swift's song "You Belong with Me" (2008) received widespread acclaim and won the MTV Video Music Award for Best Female Video.

1. Which music video by Taylor Swift features scenes set in a Mansion-themed environment?
A) "You Belong with Me"
B) "Shake It Off"
C) "Blank Space"
D) "Bad Blood"

2. What is the name of the Christmas tree farm Taylor Swift grew up on, which inspired her song "Christmas Tree Farm"?
A) Evergreen Acres
B) Pine Ridge Farm
C) Holiday Hill Farm
D) Sycamore Hill

In which year did Taylor Swift win the Grammy Award for Album of the Year for her album "Fearless"?
A) 2009
B) 2010
C) 2011
D) 2012

- She has performed at prestigious venues such as the Grammy Awards, the MTV Video Music Awards, and the Victoria's Secret Fashion Show.

- Swift's album "Lover" (2019) explored themes of love, relationships, and self-discovery.

- She has won multiple Nickelodeon Kids' Choice Awards for her music and contributions to entertainment.

- Taylor Swift has been praised for her songwriting craftsmanship, with many of her songs featuring clever wordplay and storytelling.
- She has won the American Country Countdown Awards for Female Vocalist of the Year multiple times.

"YOU CAN CLOSE YOUR EYES TO THINGS YOU DON'T WANT TO SEE, BUT YOU CAN'T CLOSE YOUR HEART TO THINGS YOU DON'T WANT TO FEEL."

- Taylor Swift

Did You Know ?

- Swift's song "I Knew You Were Trouble" (2012) showcased her experimentation with electronic and dubstep influences.
- She has been honored with the Songwriters Hall of Fame's Hal David Starlight Award for emerging songwriters.
- Taylor Swift's album "folklore" (2020) was recorded remotely during the COVID-19 pandemic with collaborator Aaron Dessner.
- She has won multiple Teen Choice Awards for her music, performances, and contributions to pop culture.
- Swift's song "Style" (2014) was praised for its production and received comparisons to the works of artists like Lana Del Rey.

Swift's Squad: A Closer Look at Taylor Swift's Celebrity Friends

In the glamorous world of Hollywood, Taylor Swift stands out not only for her chart-topping hits and captivating performances but also for her impressive circle of celebrity friends, famously dubbed "Swift's Squad." These friendships have become a defining aspect of Taylor's public persona, offering a glimpse into her supportive and inclusive nature. Let's take a closer look at some of Taylor Swift's closest celebrity friendships and the bonds that unite them.

1. Selena Gomez: The Sisterly Bond

One of Taylor Swift's most enduring friendships is with fellow singer and actress Selena Gomez. Their bond transcends the glitz and glam of the entertainment industry, rooted in mutual admiration, support, and sisterly love. From attending award shows together to celebrating each other's milestones, Taylor and Selena have stood by each other through thick and thin, inspiring fans with their unwavering friendship.

2. Ed Sheeran: The Musical Soulmates

Taylor Swift's friendship with singer-songwriter Ed Sheeran is a testament to the power of music to forge deep connections. United by their shared passion for songwriting and storytelling, Taylor and Ed have collaborated on numerous projects and shared the stage for unforgettable performances. Their bond goes beyond the spotlight, with Taylor and Ed often turning to each other for creative inspiration and emotional support.

3. Blake Lively and Ryan Reynolds: The Power Couple

Taylor Swift's friendship with actress Blake Lively and actor Ryan Reynolds is a delightful blend of Hollywood glamour and genuine camaraderie. Known for their playful banter and heartwarming gestures, Taylor, Blake, and Ryan exemplify the true essence of friendship in the spotlight. Whether it's attending star-studded events together or enjoying cozy nights in, Taylor and the power couple share a bond built on laughter, love, and shared experiences.

Did You Know ?

- She has been featured in documentaries such as "Taylor Swift: Reputation Stadium Tour" (2018) and "Taylor Swift: The 1989 World Tour Live" (2015).

- Taylor Swift has won multiple iHeartRadio Music Awards for her songs, albums, and contributions to the music industry.

- She has a strong presence in the gaming industry, with appearances in video games such as "Band Hero" and "The Sims 3: Showtime."

- Swift's album "Red" (2012) explored themes of heartbreak, love, and nostalgia, earning critical acclaim from music critics.

- She has won the MTV Europe Music Award for Best Female multiple times.

Discover Your Soundtrack: List Your Top Ten Taylor Swift Songs

On this page, jot down your top ten Taylor Swift tunes. Dive into the melodies that resonate with your soul and capture your experiences. Let Taylor's music be the backdrop to your journaling journey.

- Taylor Swift's song "Mine" (2010) debuted at number three on the Billboard Hot 100 chart, marking her highest debut at the time.

- She has won multiple People's Choice Awards for her music, acting, and philanthropic efforts.

- Swift's album "Speak Now" (2010) was inspired by her personal experiences and showcased her growth as a songwriter.

- She has been featured in Forbes' "30 Under 30" list multiple times for her achievements in music and entertainment.
- Taylor Swift's song "22" (2012) became an anthem for young adults navigating life and relationships in their twenties.

Behind Closed Doors: Inside Taylor Swift's Lavish Homes

Step into the world of luxury and sophistication as we take an exclusive peek inside the stunning homes of Taylor Swift. From sprawling estates to chic city apartments. Taylor's residences are a reflection of her impeccable taste and glamorous lifestyle. Join us as we explore the lavish interiors. breathtaking views. and hidden gems of Taylor's private sanctuaries.

I. Nashville Oasis: Southern Charm Meets Modern Elegance

Nestled amidst the lush greenery of Nashville, Tennessee, Taylor's sprawling estate exudes Southern charm with a contemporary twist. The grand facade welcomes guests into a world of luxury, with sweeping staircases, elegant chandeliers, and cozy sitting areas adorned with plush furnishings. Explore the spacious living rooms, state-of-the-art kitchen, and charming outdoor spaces where Taylor entertains friends and family in style.

2. New York City Penthouse: Sky-High Sophistication

Perched high above the bustling streets of New York City, Taylor's penthouse offers panoramic views of the iconic skyline and Hudson River. Step inside to discover sleek modern design, with floor-to-ceiling windows, sleek marble countertops, and minimalist decor. The open-concept layout seamlessly blends living and entertaining spaces, while private terraces provide the perfect retreat for taking in the city lights.

3. Coastal Retreat: Tranquility by the Sea

Escape to Taylor's coastal retreat, where sun-drenched beaches and ocean breezes create an atmosphere of serenity and relaxation. The beachfront property boasts expansive decks, infinity pools, and lush gardens overlooking the sparkling waters of the ocean. Inside, airy interiors are adorned with nautical accents, natural materials, and cozy furnishings, offering a serene coastal getaway for Taylor and her guests.

4. English Countryside Manor: Old-World Charm meets Modern Luxury

Immerse yourself in the timeless beauty of Taylor's English countryside manor, where rolling hills, manicured gardens, and ivy-covered walls create a picture-perfect setting straight out of a fairy tale. Step through the grand entrance to discover elegant period details, luxurious furnishings, and cozy fireplaces that evoke a sense of old-world charm and sophistication. Explore the sprawling grounds, tranquil ponds, and secret gardens that make this estate a true English gem.

Song Reflections: Select a Taylor Swift song that resonates with you emotionally. Write a journal entry reflecting on why the song is meaningful to you and how it makes you feel.

Date:

_____

_____

_____

_____

_____

_____

_____

_____

_____

_____

_____

_____

_____

_____

_____

_____

"IF YOU'RE LUCKY ENOUGH
TO BE DIFFERENT, DON'T
EVER CHANGE."

- Taylor Swift

- She has won the Juno Award for International Album of the Year for her contributions to the Canadian music market.
- Swift's album "Fearless" (2008) won the Grammy Award for Best Country Album and received critical acclaim for its storytelling and production.
- She has collaborated with renowned photographers and directors on music videos and visual projects.
- Taylor Swift's song "The Story of Us" (2010) explored themes of love and heartbreak, drawing inspiration from personal experiences.
- She has been featured on the cover of Rolling Stone magazine multiple times throughout her career.

Create Your Own Lyrics: Use Taylor
Swift's songs as inspiration to write
your own lyrics. Channel your
thoughts and emotions into creating
a song of your own.

Date:

_____

_____

_____

_____

_____

_____

_____

_____

_____

_____

_____

_____

_____

_____

_____

_____

"THE ONLY ONE WHO CAN TELL YOU 'YOU CAN'T' IS YOU. AND YOU DON'T HAVE TO LISTEN."

- **Taylor Swift**

- Swift's album "evermore" (2020) featured collaborations with indie artists such as Bon Iver and The National.
- She has won multiple Billboard Women in Music Awards for her contributions to the music industry.
- Taylor Swift's song "Mean" (2010) addressed criticism and bullying, encouraging listeners to rise above negativity.
- She has performed at major music festivals around the world, including Lollapalooza and the Bonnaroo Music Festival.
- Swift's album "Speak Now" (2010) was nominated for Album of the Year at the Grammy Awards, solidifying her status as a songwriter and performer.

Taylor Swift's Secret Diary: Imagine
you found Taylor Swift's secret diary.
What do you think she would write
about? Write a pretend entry from
Taylor's diary about one of her
exciting adventures.

Date:

_____

_____

_____

_____

_____

_____

_____

_____

_____

_____

_____

_____

_____

_____

_____

_____

"

I THINK FEARLESS IS HAVING
FEARS BUT JUMPING
ANYWAY

- Taylor Swift

- She has been honored with the Nashville Songwriters Association International (NSAI) Songwriter-Artist of the Decade Award.
- Taylor Swift's song "White Horse" (2008) won the Grammy Award for Best Country Song and Best Female Country Vocal Performance.
- She has won multiple MTV Europe Music Awards for her music videos and contributions to pop culture.

- Swift's album "1989" (2014) featured collaborations with hitmakers such as Max Martin, Shellback, and Jack Antonoff.
- She has been praised for her live performances, which often feature elaborate staging and choreography.

Behind the Lyrics: Exploring Taylor Swift's Songwriting Secrets

Taylor Swift's songwriting is a journey into the depths of human emotion, weaving stories that resonate with listeners worldwide. Each song is a chapter in her life, filled with personal experiences, heartbreaks, and triumphs. Let's take a closer look at the secrets behind Taylor Swift's captivating songwriting process.

Unveiling Inspiration

Taylor Swift draws inspiration from her own life, turning moments of joy, pain, and everything in between into lyrical masterpieces. Whether it's a fleeting romance, a heartfelt apology, or a nostalgic reflection, Taylor's songs are deeply rooted in her personal experiences. By opening up about her own life, Taylor creates a connection with her audience that transcends boundaries and speaks to the universal human experience.

Crafting Melodies

Behind every Taylor Swift song is a meticulously crafted melody that complements the emotion and message of the lyrics. Taylor's songs range from stripped-down acoustic ballads to upbeat pop anthems, showcasing her versatility as a songwriter and musician. With each chord progression and vocal arrangement, Taylor creates a sonic landscape that draws listeners in and leaves a lasting impression.

Navigating Themes

Taylor Swift's music explores a wide range of themes, from love and heartbreak to friendship, empowerment, and self-discovery. Through her lyrics, Taylor delves into the complexities of human relationships, offering insights into the highs and lows of love and life. Whether she's singing about the thrill of new romance or the pain of betrayal, Taylor's honesty and vulnerability shine through in every word.

Unlocking Emotions

At the heart of Taylor Swift's songwriting is a deep well of emotion that resonates with listeners of all ages. Her ability to capture the essence of human experience and convey it through music is what sets her apart as a songwriter. Whether she's expressing joy, sorrow, anger, or hope. Taylor's lyrics are always raw, authentic, and relatable, making her music a source of comfort and inspiration for millions of fans around the world.

In a Nutshell

As we peel back the layers of Taylor Swift's songwriting process, we gain a deeper appreciation for the artistry and emotion that infuse her music. Each song is a testament to Taylor's talent, creativity, and unwavering commitment to storytelling. Through her music, Taylor invites us to share in her journey, reminding us that we're never alone in our triumphs and tribulations.

Did You Know ?

- Taylor Swift's song "Back to December" (2010) addressed regrets and apologies, showcasing her emotional depth as a songwriter.
- She has won multiple Brit Awards for her music and contributions to the British music industry.
- Swift's album "Speak Now" (2010) featured singles such as "Mine," "Back to December," and "Mean," which received critical acclaim and commercial success.
- She has been recognized by the Guinness World Records for various achievements in music and entertainment.
- Taylor Swift's song "Sparks Fly" (2010) became a fan favorite and was later included as a single on her album "Speak Now."

"I'VE FOUND TIME CAN HEAL MOST ANYTHING, AND YOU JUST MIGHT FIND WHO YOU'RE SUPPOSED TO BE."

- Taylor Swift

- She has won multiple Academy of Country Music Awards for her music, performances, and contributions to the country music genre.

- Swift's album "Fearless" (2008) included hit singles such as "Love Story," "You Belong with Me," and "Fearless," which catapulted her to international fame.

- She has been featured in Time magazine's list of the 100 Most Influential People in the World multiple times.

- Taylor Swift's song "Ours" (2011) became a radio hit and was praised for its relatable lyrics and catchy melody.

- She has won multiple Grammy Awards for her music, including Album of the Year, Song of the Year, and Best Pop Vocal Album.

Gratitude Journal: Write down three things you're grateful for today. It could be something related to Taylor Swift, like her music making you happy, or something else entirely.

Date:

_____

_____

_____

_____

_____

_____

_____

_____

_____

_____

_____

_____

_____

_____

_____

_____

Made in the USA
Monee, IL
06 March 2024

54580601R00049